And They

All Lived

Happily

Ever After

And They All Lived Happily Ever After

Lessons For Writing Your Book of Life

And They All Lived Happily Ever After

FOR INFORMATION CONTACT:
LaJoyce Martin
202 South First Street
Morris, Oklahoma 74445

Printed in the USA by

MORRIS PUBLISHING

3212 East Highway 30 • Kearney, NE 68847 • 1-800-650-7888

Oh that my words were now written!
oh that they were printed in a book!

Job 19:23

Table of Contents

Introduction

A book of life I'm writing
But not with ink and pen;
My thoughts and words and actions
Are written down therein.

Oh, care I take and caution
That the pages proper be!
For my Publisher in Heaven
My Finished Work will see.

— L.M.

"A writer must have his heart in the art."
— Source Unknown

Chapter One

The Pages in Between ☞

There I was again. . . .

In the corner of the prayer room. Draped over the same orange plastic chair. Depreciating the carpet with the toes of my outsized shoes.

My troubled thoughts clotted into words that formed a prayer (albeit a pitiful excuse for one). "Lord," I said, "I know You promised to be the Author and Finisher of my faith, but what about *those pages in between*? That's what has me worried!"

The pages in between: Those are the x number of days in our lives sandwiched between the time we are born and the time we leave this world. The ordinary days.

When we're grouchy. When we burn the toast. When the dog chews up the newspaper with the coupons in it. When we want to pull our hair–and everyone else's, too. The Mondays. The sick days. The year-long days just before payday.

The days that turn to weeks that turn to months that turn to years. The years that turn our hair gray, make our bones brittle and slide our teeth under the bridge.

"We spend our years as a tale that is told," the Book of Psalms says, letting us know that each of our lives is a story. Everyone is writing a book!

It would be nice if God would write every syllable of our lives for us, wouldn't it? But, unfortunately, that isn't the case. He isn't a ghostwriter (someone who writes for and in the name of another person). Much of life's script is left up to us.

What do our lives' books contain? Our works (Revelation 20:12) and our words (Matthew 12:36) are recorded there. That I had the responsibility of those "in between" pages was a jolting revelation to me. My life–a *book*?

Yes. Every human ever born is writing a book. The saved and the unsaved. The unrighteous "write grievousness which they have prescribed" (Isaiah 10:1), and woe is decreed unto them. Their books "shall be stubble: and the day that cometh shall burn them up" according to Malachi 4:1. They are spending a lifetime of "writing" for nothing.

But good news! The born again child of God is writing a different book! We are writing books for the Master. At the end of each of our lives' stories, we want to hear Him say, "Well done, thou good and faithful servant

. . . enter thou into the joy of thy lord" (Matthew 25:21). We want our books to end up on Heaven's bookshelf.

Of course, we are not writing the stories of our lives with pen and paper. We're writing with thoughts and deeds and attitudes, but they are just as indelible as printer's ink. God, Who determines the worth of our books, reads them. "I know your works," He said to all seven of the churches in Revelation. He knows ours, too.

As I studied the rules for writing a book for an earthly market, I was amazed by the parallel to the process of "writing" my spiritual book. The instructions from my writing classes lent themselves so perfectly to my walk with God that it boggled my mind! Indeed, I found such a rich analogy that I wanted to share it. You might find some pointers, some guidelines that would help you with your "story." I hope that you do; that is the intent of my efforts.

So what is the purpose of our "tale that is told"? Some authors write for fun. Is that the reason for our spiritual books? No. Others write for financial gain. Is that our goal? A thousand times no. Still others write for self-gratification. Is that our objective? No again.

It is to have our work accepted by the Master on Judgment Day that we strive. "But in every nation he that feareth him, and worketh righteousness, is accepted with him" (Acts 10:35).

My life story will be different from yours. It is even

unlike my husband's. He would be pleased to help God push up the sun each morning and then rush to the coffee shop as soon as it opens for breakfast. I like my Frosted Mini-Wheats at the crack of noon. He has blue eyes. Mine are green. He drives in the middle of his lane. I hug the right shoulder.

Have you ever found two books at the library–written by different authors–that were identical? Nor have I. Likewise, no two life stories will be alike.

You may have a voice like a nightingale. I haven't. Or a knack for decorating the church. I don't. Or perhaps you can make a tambourine dance. I can't.

That's why the Lord told us that comparing ourselves to someone else isn't smart (II Corinthians 10:12). I may be writing my life's story on a third grade level while yours is much more advanced. Yours may have finer print than mine. Mine may be shorter or longer than yours.

Neither are we free to criticize another because his abilities do not measure up to our own. Indeed, if we are as busy working on our own lives as we should be, we won't have time to mind the business of anyone else.

Why we write (our motives) and *how* we write determine our eternal destiny. *What* we write matters, too. We are free to put in or leave out what we wish. God gave us that right. We can put in prayer or leave it out. We can put in complaining or leave it out. We can put in chastity or leave it out, and the list goes on.

Not all chapters of our lives will be pleasant. There have been pages in my own life's book that I balked at recording. Sometimes I didn't even like the plot. I wish I could have skipped the chapters . . .

. . . when my teenage daughters were in an automobile accident and my youngest lapsed into a no brain response coma. . . . when I was on my hands and knees for sixty-six days and nights with a back injury. . . . when a dear friend died with cancer.

Who wants electric bills, taxes or leaking radiators? Who wants backslidden kids, parents with Alzheimer's or neighbors with noisy dogs?

I learned early that it isn't enough to be infatuated with the idea, the charisma, of recording an "experience." Writing for the Master isn't just a hobby. Without a genuine love for the truth, we will abandon the chore of daily diligent penmanship for an easier task.

A writer must have his heart in the art. Do I really want to be a masterpiece for God? At any cost? Do I want it *with all my heart*? Do I treasure my daily walk with God? "For where your treasure is, there will your heart be also" (Luke 12:34).

You've heard the statement, "He has his heart set on thus and so." It might be going to college, buying a boat or getting married. Where one's heart is riveted shows up in one's thoughts, one's conversation, one's lifestyle. What do I think about? Talk about? Plan around? Earth and earthly things, or heaven and heavenly things?

The first and great commandment for writing your life's story is found in Matthew 22:37. Jesus said it. "Thou shalt love the Lord thy God with all thy heart, and with all thy soul, and with all thy mind."

Writing instructors tell us there are only three basic requirements to produce a good work. You must want to write clearly. You must be willing to work hard. You must know and follow some basic guidelines. Cannot these apply spiritually?

"Don't write anything you cannot put your soul into," teachers insist. "Find a subject you care about. It is this caring and not your game with language that will be the most compelling element in your work."

What do I care most about? Is it my job? My grandchildren? My coin collection? My Jeep? Or is the thing that compels me my love for God? The results of my story are herein determined.

Haven't we all seen it? An individual swept up in the excitement of a big revival. The song. The shout. The dynamics. But when the revival is over, the evangelist gone and it is back to Wednesday Bible study, where are they?

The sun withered them because they had no root. Or without enough "earth," they wilted. Or they were choked by circumstances that pricked and gouged. (Parable, Matthew 13:5-7)

The New Testament's fifth book gives the account of a man whose heart was not where it should have been. Simon, the sorcerer (my kids called him Simon, the saucer), was immensely impressed with Brother Philip, the flaming evangelist. Wow! Those healings! Those miracles!

As Peter and John placed their hands on the seekers, they received the gift of the Holy Ghost. Wow! That power!

Ah! Simon, a clever magician, wanted that forte. He relished the thought of being center stage with the spotlight focused on himself. He craved the ambrosia of hero worship. What a fun life story! How self-fulfilling!

Quite suddenly, his true colors began to emerge. He plopped a bag of money at Apostle Peter's feet. "What will you take for it?"

"Take for what?"

"For that power. For that laying-on-of-hands secret. I want to work miracles. I want that authority. Just name your price—"

Uh-oh. The story is getting off track. It isn't written for the glory of God but by a self-seeker interested in his own fame.

Peter's dander flew. "You and your money can both get lost! Your heart is not in it!" The old fisherman's blazing rebuke almost heats the page in the eighth chapter of Acts.

If I am writing my life's book for my own glory, my own aggrandizement or any reason other than to glorify Christ, my heart is not in the art. I am writing in vain, for the Lord will reject my work.

At the beginning of a writing class in which I was enrolled, the professor asked us to participate in a self-analysis. Some of the questions posed were these: What do you love to do? What can you continue to do? What people do you admire? What issue burns within you?

The answers to these questions gave the professor an insight into our "heart." Every now and then, a time of reflection and spiritual analysis will help us keep the pages in between attuned to the proper spiritual emphasis. It will reveal our priorities, our motives.

Why am I putting all this effort into my life's book? What is my goal, my story, in a single sentence? Am I really putting my heart into the art?

We are all writers, filling the pages in between here and the rapture with something trivial or something worthwhile. What have I written today? Would I be ashamed to hand my draft to the Master?

Chapter Two

Get the Sky Right ✍

Patsy sat across from me in eighth grade study hall. She was a genius! Her Number 2 yellow pencil could do tricks!

On her notebook paper, she would slant a mark to the right for a forehead, make a half heart for a cheek and a right slash for a chin. She would add a blob of hair, killer eyelashes, a nose and mouth, and zippo! In mere seconds, she had created "somebody."

Simple enough. Anyone could do that. So I picked up my Number 2 pencil (mine was yellow, too). Surely it would perform the same magic. A straaaaight line . . . a haaaalf heart . . . a right slaaaash . . . Who would my "somebody" look like?

But, lo! My pencil rebelled. My indistinguishable somebody didn't look like anything or anybody! It brought

19

me great chagrin and the rude awakening that talents are not parceled out equally.

I was quite depressed until I learned that I could take mere words and make mental pictures. Cozy fireplaces. Rustic cabins. Dogwood blossoms. I didn't need lines and curves and blobs of hair.

A block to the north and three blocks east lived a little boy, about eight or nine years old, who read anything he could get his hands on. He and I were a whole generation apart, my birthday ushering me into the envied world of teens. Besides, I was already in the six foot tall bracket, and he still dwelt in the four foot era.

I wrote a moronic story about a house that had seven gables and gave it to him to read. He loved it, and he begged for more! He digested everything I wrote, greatly inflating my thirteen-year-old ego. The shine in his eyes was enough to keep my pencil busy.

In all fairness, I should mention that most of our neighborhood lived on a poverty level, and my young fan was literally starved for reading material. He likely had never owned a book, and libraries were unheard of in West Texas towns that squatted in cotton patches. (Those of you who have been there know I speak the truth!) There wasn't a library in our entire county. My idiotic stories had no competition.

By the time I was a senior in high school, I was feeling my oats enough to enter a writing contest sponsored by the Daughters of the American Revolution. My essay won honorable mention. But as I look back, I suspect everyone else's did, too.

Life sped on, bringing me a job. Then a husband. Then three youngsters. I wrote some "little stuff" for publishers desperate for material, but I hadn't the time to start my book.

Then, when my girls were old enough to put crooked bows in their own hair and my son could make jelly sandwiches, I knew it was time to begin. I must put it off no longer.

It wasn't easy, that first book. It was, in fact, a fight to the finish. There were delays, discouragements, distractions. I sometimes doubted my ability, my durability, and my "stickability." The work was painfully slow. Would I ever be able to complete a whole book?

Maybe I expected it to be less difficult to write a book. Perhaps I thought it wouldn't take so much time and effort. So much concentration. So much dedication. Why didn't someone tell me that writing a book wasn't candy and roses, but that it was hard work and exasperation? Long days and short nights. Mental sweat and tears.

I'm glad Paul warned me in his letters that my living for God wouldn't be all music and candles. He honestly foretold that I would face hard times in the writing of my life story (II Timothy 2:3) and that it would be a battle to the end (I Timothy 6:12).

Paul was being realistic. A Christian life isn't all sugar. Read carefully the recipe for a fine chocolate cake. Study the ingredients one by one. There is the chocolate, of course. Taste a little crumb that falls off the bar. It is bitter. And sour milk? A whole cup? Then comes the awful soda that your mother gave you for a stomachache. Vanilla flavoring yet. It smells good, but it tastes terrible. Can any good come from these bitter ingredients?

A life for God calls for some "bitter" ingredients. Self-denial. Sacrifice. Flesh fighting. If I pay tithes, I can't buy a new outfit. Missionaries? That makes *three* offerings! A *skirt* in gym class when everyone else is wearing sweats?

How would the chocolate cake taste if those disagreeable ingredients were left out? How would my Christianity "taste" without self-discipline? Trust God, and keep "writing." The finished product will be worth the struggle.

Oh, certainly, the humanity that we are will fuss and fume. It's too cold to go to midweek service. I have a runner in my hose. I can't find my glasses. The Avon lady is coming by, and I need deodorant.

The devil will try to knock the pen from your hand every day. He will tell you that you'll never complete your book for God anyway. He may send a messenger of affliction to buffet you as he did Paul or use scare tactics, ridicule, opposition and craft (Nehemiah). Or he may bring sore troubles (Job). He doesn't want your book of life to be a volume for God's glory. He didn't want you to start it, he doesn't want you to continue it, and he surely doesn't plan for you to complete it.

I'm afraid we weaken the Christian life when we portray it as a journey free from the bullets and arrows of outrageous fortune. Christians, working on their spiritual manuscripts, are real people faced with real disappointments and real setbacks that must be overcome. We just have a real God to help us!

"We are troubled on every side, yet not distressed; we are perplexed, but not in despair; Persecuted, but not forsaken; cast down, but not destroyed" (II Corinthians 4:8,9).

Nothing but pure dedication can see one through the wretched stresses and pitfalls of a spiritual writer to the final rewards at book's end. No child of God who is really committed will be discouraged by the difficulties. No other sort of person can be encouraged enough to stay with the task.

Faith that can be lost over some circumstance of life is not Bible faith. Faith isn't a good luck charm or a glorified rabbit's foot. The giants of faith–Abraham, Joseph, Noah and others–had problems and trials aplenty. They didn't lose their faith when things went awry. Nothing or no one can kill real faith.

God didn't promise that our faith would exempt us

from heartaches. He isn't a good-natured Santa Claus handing out goodies on the street. But faith does help us keep writing through our tears, and it stays with us to project's end where real life will begin.

A young artist labored over his first landscape painting, striving to get it just right. He worked and worked, but something was missing.

"What am I doing wrong?" he asked an old veteran artist.

"Son, in any landscape scene, you have to get the sky right first," the elderly gentleman counseled. "When the horizon is right, everything will fall into place."

This is our secret to a successful Christian life. Each morning when I rise, I must go to God and get enough "sky" upon which to brush my earthly scene for that day.

When my readers read what I have written, I want them to be able to see the "sky" in it. If all they see are earthly objects, my picture isn't right.

So what if they see your new car? Your manicured lawn? Your Rolex? Your sports trophy on the mantel? If they haven't seen Jesus, you have let them down.

Who is reading over your shoulder? Your nephew? Your employer? The checker at Wal-Mart? Will they see enough "sky" today?

If I fail in my horizon, I have failed. The writing of my life's book falls short of the perspective it needs.

Mountains are never too tall nor rivers too wide in

our "picture" if the sky has been painted first, for then everything is proportioned to the world above. The right amount of heaven gives our work the right amount of harmony.

Take care of the horizon first today–then write like mad!

Chapter Three

Ready, Set, Go! ✍

How should I start my book? In deep thought, I chew on the end of my pencil and draw my brows together.

Shall it be: "Memory called up last Saturday's drama and presented it in one grand replay"? Or is that too stilted? Too vague? Too frilly? It might be better to begin: "He remembered exactly where he was last Saturday."

Oh, how I agonize over a book's first sentence! I write and think and rewrite and think some more. It has to be *right*. Not nearly right. Exactly right.

Every writer knows that the first paragraph may well be the most important of your book. Some writers spend as much time on their initial few lines as they do on the whole story. They realize that one's beginning can spell success or failure.

27

"Begin with the moment or day that made a difference," advises my notes from *The Fabric of Writing* class. Great advice.

Remember the moment you began your book for the Lord? The first word, first sentence, first paragraph? It may have been when someone knocked on your door. It may have been the moment you stepped into a Spirit led church. It may have been when you read a certain verse in the Bible. Whatever your beginning, it was the day that made the difference. Were you kneeling at an altar? Sitting? Standing? Whatever your position, that day (or night) was like no other. You were changed!

"Therefore if any man be in Christ, he is a new creature: old things are passed away; behold, all things are become new" (II Corinthians 5:17).

What a place to start! With conversion. That part has to be right. Not nearly right. Exactly right.

That's where the one hundred and twenty in the upper room (Acts, chapter 2) began writing their brand-new books, copyrighted circa A.D. 33. Such openers! "And they were all filled with the Holy Ghost, and began to speak with other tongues, as the Spirit gave them utterance" (Acts 2:4). Can't you just imagine some of their first sentences?

"I'd been there for ten days–and then it happened!"

"I heard this mighty 'whooshing' sound burst into the room."

28

"Suddenly, my tongue took leave of its native language as a glowing, V-shaped flame appeared from nowhere and hovered above my head."

"The mob that gathered below our window said we certainly weren't acting like Galileans. . . ."

"*What will The Jerusalem News say about this?* I wondered."

"I was accused of being drunk, but I wasn't."

"Peter saved the day for us."

Any one of these introductions would have made us want to read more, wouldn't it? Three thousand additional souls began their books that day when they heard the wonderful works of God.

The books of our spiritual lives begin with our personal Pentecost. Like those in the upper room, we can tell it in such a way that the world wants to know more.

My own father could have started his story like this: "What was I doing at a *ladies'* prayer meeting? I was desperate to receive this gift that I had heard about! One sister was telling me to hold on, and another said to turn loose. Hold on? Turn loose? As I tuned out both of them and tuned into heaven, the glory of God fell upon me!"

My husband's grandmother might begin her book: "I sat my bucket down by the cow pen gate. That's where it happened! All the chickens, horses and cows knew when I got the Holy Ghost!"

My father-in-law's manuscript started this way:

"Until I was nine years old, I didn't know God was anything but a curse word. Saying it earned me a whipping. Then a brush arbor meeting came to town, and at a small, wooden altar, I learned that God could transform a child's heart and mind by His Spirit."

"In a big church at a big altar in a big town, I had my big day," my husband would tell you. "It was the last night of a revival, and I knew the Lord would fill me that night. I spoke in tongues for an hour and a half. I gave out before God did!"

A cousin the nearest my age had an unforgettable onset at age ten: "The next morning after my encounter with God, I picked up my spoon to eat my Post Toasties. When I opened my mouth to ask for something, I couldn't speak English. I was still under the influence of heaven's language."

"For they heard them speak with tongues, and magnify God" (Acts 10:46).

With my head in my Sunday School teacher's lap and pigtails hanging to the hardwood floor, I picked up my "pen" to record my walk with God at an early age. I was baptized in the Name of Jesus in a mud bottomed lake at age six. What a day!

Begin with the moment or day that made a difference. If the day of conversion didn't make a difference in your life, you had no conversion. To do a Christian's work with a sinner's feelings would be bondage. But our feelings are revolutionized, and now we delight in the God of our salvation!

Some of us started our books at a tender age, others after tucking away many birthdays. But there's one thing you can bank on; young or old, there are no dull and boring beginnings for a born again Christian.

You may not have been knocked down on the road to Damascus, seen a blinding light or heard a voice calling your name from the sky, but you can say, "Clean! That's how I felt when the Holy Ghost came in. And such peace! Such joy!"

"For the kingdom of God is not meat and drink; but righteousness, and peace, and joy in the Holy Ghost" (Romans 14:17).

Chapter Four

Rules, Rules and More Rules ✍

I'll never forget a scathing letter I got from an editor for not obeying one of his cardinal rules when submitting a story. It concerned my responsibility for postage. I learned the hard way that publishers have rules, and writers are not free to disregard them.

Back in the old typewriter days, one of our first commandments was: *Clean your keys before preparing your manuscript.* It was written on the tablets of our minds. Failure to keep the commandment was unthinkable.

Back in the old days of Pentecost, we heard a lot about cleaning up our lives when we started for heaven. It was written on the tablets of our souls: *Repent.* Failure to do so was unthinkable.

Repentance was the password. Clean your slate of worldliness. Turn your back on unrighteousness. Unholy dress and actions. Bywords. Worldly amusements. Unwholesome literature. (Worldliness seemed to include more items back then.) If we weren't willing to "clean our keys," we weren't ready to start our books.

My husband was removing the priceless front doors from a century old denominational church in Dallas, Texas. In the building were found some church minutes dated prior to 1899. A list of forbidden sins included dancing, being drunk, suing a fellow member in civil court, going to the show, swearing, swindling, domestic troubles, and being the leader of a baseball league. That interesting bit of history shows that not only do buildings deteriorate over the years, but so values do, also.

Yet genuine repentance is still one of God's rules. David knew that his having clean "keys" was important to God. That's why he penned, "Create in me a clean heart, O God; and renew a right spirit within me" (Psalm 51:10). He wanted to get off on the right foot with his Publisher.

In the book of Revelation, the Lamb's Bride was arrayed in fine linen, clean and white (Revelation 19:8). This is the Publisher's rule. (Some editors even require a certain grade of paper.)

Editors will not accept sloppy work. Why should God? They require clean work with a new ribbon, bold enough not to create a faint image. They are particular in this, and it is only reasonable to obey. Who wants to spend time writing a book that will not be accepted?

The apostles, as well as our forefathers in the faith, used bold print. Paul and Barnabas waxed bold (Acts 13:46). Peter and James made it a matter of prayer: "Grant unto thy servants, that with all boldness they may speak thy word" (Acts 4:30). No weak, faded ribbons for these two!

Another important editorial rule highlighting a marvelous spiritual lesson is this: Leave adequate margins on both sides of your copy, as well as at top and bottom. My six-year-old grandson could interpret that. He'd say, "Stay away from the edges!"

In the "good old days" (before computers), we set our own typing margins. Nobody wanted to be disqualified for running outside the marginal limits of the page. A bell would ding when we got dangerously close to the border.

In our modern society with modern equipment and modern technology, the old typewriter's warning bell is gone, and the new machines justify everything. You don't have to worry about having to change lines or pages.

For the secular world, the results of modernization are a welcomed change, but in the spirit realm, we still need a warning system, a bell that dings in our consciences when we get too close to the edge and run over into world-liness. Dare we switch to a new program that justifies our wrongdoings? By no means! When we begin to make excuses to fulfil the lusts of the flesh, we are crossing God's boundaries.

"Thus saith the LORD, Stand ye in the ways, and see, and ask for the old paths, where is the good way, and walk therein, and ye shall find rest for your souls" (Jeremiah 6:16).

Here's a good one. Publishing rules state that the copy must be printed on one side of the page only. Take note that this means no double-sided, two-faced stuff.

There was probably more than one reason for this stipulation. With the older type printing, wording on the back would bleed through to distort the front. It would make the copy messy and hard to read. Also, one-sidedness made reading faster and easier for the editor. He didn't have to turn the pages over to see what might be behind.

Now and then we meet individuals who flatter us to our faces and criticize us to our backs. Such a person is breaking editorial etiquette. He/she is writing on both sides of the paper. The result? Rejection of the manuscript. "In so doing," Job says, "my Maker would soon take me away" (Job 32:22).

Pages, say the guidelines, also must be submitted in consecutive order. Ah, what a lesson for the book of life! I cannot skip over to tomorrow or turn back to yesterday. Yesterday is dead, tomorrow unborn. Today is my assignment.

One of my pet peeves is to read a book with pages missing. Nothing makes sense when there is a gap between page 56 and page 59. Likewise, in my Christian experience, I can't shirk the duties of the present, skipping chores that I don't enjoy, and expect the future to make sense. I can't lay down my cross at age 16 and pick it up again at 25 without damaging my book's continuity. "If ye continue in my word," Jesus said (John 8:31), "then are ye my disciples indeed."

Keep your book in order. Just write this day with all your heart. When it is time for the next page, do the same for it.

Neatness is vital in the preparation of your life's manuscript. Smudged pages? Spots? Fingerprints? These bring frowns instead of smiles to those who view your work.

God has told us that He will not tolerate spots or smudges in our lives' books. He insists on our best work. "That he might present it to himself a glorious church, not having spot, or wrinkle, or any such thing; but that it should be holy and without blemish" (Ephesians 5:27).

When we have all these rules firmly fixed in our minds, we can then concentrate on the story itself. What will make the script better? Clearer? Some phrases take away from the story's beauty. Some things we say and do need to be left out entirely since our lives are "known and read of all men" (II Corinthians 3:2).

Remember, we are not writing our books for ourselves but for God. "That ye should shew forth the praises of him who hath called you out of darkness into his marvellous light" (I Peter 2:9). He's the Great Publisher.

"Many writers start out thinking in terms of what *they* want to write," says the *Writer's Digest*, "and not in terms of what editors want. That is what keeps so many writers unpublished for so long."

What does God want? Clean lives. Bold messages. Single-mindedness. Spotless, unwrinkled spirits, free from the fingerprints of this world.

Anything else? Yes, here's one last "rule." God reserves the privilege of choosing the title and cover design of your life's book. According to an established Christian press, a publisher holds the right by contract to make that choice.

Do you suppose Jeremiah *wanted* to weep his life away for his nation? Would Paul have chosen stripes and imprisonment in a Roman jail? Would the early martyrs have picked a life of wandering about in sheepskins and goatskins, destitute, afflicted and tormented?

It isn't likely. But they didn't argue with the Master's design for their books of life. What has He chosen for me to write? My title? My cover?

The design God chooses for me is best. If I submit to His will, He can exclaim with joy, "That one turned out just like I planned!"

Chapter Five

No Conflict,
No Story ✍🏻

So all our chapters will be uplifting, happy and exciting, right? Wrong!

Our books of life deal in reality with "this side of paradise" problems. We lost our contact lenses and can't see to read the directions on the medicine bottle. The heating unit goes out during the snow storm. Our lawn mower is stolen. The drain pipe springs a leak. Mice get in the pantry and eat the instant oatmeal.

Some chapters will be hard and tough. There have been whole weeks in my life that I thought I couldn't live through. They were tearjerkers (my own tears). There were black moments when hope seemed lost, and my whole book of life read like a miserable paradox.

Once we were dismissed from a church we loved.

Another time our baby had a raging fever in a strange town, in a tiny travel trailer with no telephone. We have been caught in a blizzard miles from human help.

Jesus warned us. He said we would have troubles in this world. "In the world ye shall have tribulation: but be of good cheer; I have overcome the world" (John 16:33).

Peter warned us. He advised us not to think these troubles abnormal. "Beloved, think it not strange concerning the fiery trial which is to try you, as though some strange thing happened to you: But rejoice, inasmuch as ye are partakers of Christ's sufferings; that, when his glory shall be revealed, ye may be glad also with exceeding joy" (I Peter 4:12,13).

Paul also warned us. He said the hard times were for our good. That tribulation worketh patience; and patience, experience; and experience, hope: and hope maketh not ashamed (Romans 5:3-5).

If I heard it in the writing seminars once, I heard it a dozen times. *Where there is no conflict, there is no story.* The teachers pounded it into our heads!

Oh, yes, Paul's spiritual volume began with a great, happy, exciting start. A bright light! A voice from the sky! A wondrous revelation! Then (why can't the text stay pretty?) came the conflict. He was beaten three times. Stoned once. Survived three shipwrecks. Spent hours in a murky sea. Faced perils, perils and more perils. Weariness. Pain. (Why pain?) Hunger. Thirst. Cold. He was often hatless and coatless.

If conflict is necessary to a story, we will agree that Paul had the proper ingredients. In overwhelming proportions. But what a story his was!

Now think of your favorite Bible characters. Joseph? Queen Esther? Daniel? You will find that each of the heroes of faith had a generous share of conflict. They had the makings of a story.

Conflict is something pushing back. If you go from the front porch to the picket fence and there are no obstacles, there is no conflict. But if you trip over a toy in the yard, stub your toe on a root or skid in a mud puddle very nearly breaking your neck, you then have a story. Don't you see? If you are ground down by circumstances and you aren't pushing back, there is no conflict.

Even thirty second commercials have conflict. Some of you will recall with me the ancient, sing-song radio advertisement for a soap called Rinso-White. The detergent had to fight dirt and grime to get the clothes clean.

My sister-in-law wanted to enter a writing contest. She couldn't tell how to fix hair, bake a pie or paint on pottery. There was no "story" in these activities although she was versed in all of them. She needed conflict. So she wrote about her toddler. Was he a mild, orderly, always obedient child? No.

She rescued him from the middle of a busy highway,

fished him from the bottom of a water-filled baptistry and snatched him from his dance on the cracked lid of a well. These conflicts stood between her and her getting this child to adulthood. (She did get him there!) Her story, threaded with breathtaking conflict, won a first prize.

What stands between you and heaven? An unsaved companion? A community with no truth teaching church? A physical disability that threatens your faith?

The greater the obstacle, the more glory in over-coming it. The greatest spiritual benefits come in our storms. When we are finished with our lives' stories, we may thank God more for the trials along our journeys than for some of the experiences that pleased us.

In journalism we studied different types of conflict. They are categorized as:

Man against nature. (Paul's storm at sea in Acts 27)

Man against self, internal conflict. (Elijah on Horeb in I Kings 19)

Man against time. (Saul's impatience in I Samuel 13)

Man against society. (Jesus and the Pharisees in Matthew 12)

Man against man. (David and Goliath in I Samuel 17)

Man against God. (Jonah in Jonah, chapter 1)

Somewhere in your own life's book, each of these types of controversy will likely be realized, for God will have overcomers. Without conflict, there would be nothing to overcome. How many times did the Lord repeat the words "to him that overcometh" in the New Testament's final book?

Those who overcome the conflicts in their earthly walks are promised an impressive array of goodies:

Fruit from the Tree of Life. (Revelation 2:7)
A white stone with a brand-new name. (Rev. 2:17)
Power over nations. (Rev. 2:26)
To be made a pillar in the temple of God. (Rev. 3:12)
A seat with God on His throne. (Rev. 3:21)

Conflict exposes character. It is not ease but hardship that makes men. We learn things about ourselves when we are placed under extreme stress. The best or worst comes to the surface in times of duress. We become bitter or better. Larger or smaller. Richer or poorer.

Each trial we overcome contributes to our spiritual growth, increases our faith and gives us our testimonies. "That the trial of your faith, being much more precious than of gold that perisheth, though it be tried with fire, might be found unto praise and honour and glory at the appearing of Jesus Christ" (I Peter 1:7).

On the merchant's shelf, a story without conflict will sit. It won't be a million copy seller. In fact, it likely won't stay in circulation for very long. It has little literary merit since action proceeds only from characters in conflict. It is but an anecdote and not a story.

Amos pronounced woe upon a people who were "at ease in Zion," shielding themselves from all conflict. They, he said, would be removed by God from "circulation."

Since I don't wish to sit on a shelf and collect dust, I must join Paul in his conclusion: "Most gladly therefore will I rather glory in my infirmities, that the power of Christ may rest upon me" (II Corinthians 12:9).

Why should we shrink from struggle in our lives' books, knowing that "our light affliction, which is but for a moment, worketh for us a far more exceeding and eternal weight of glory" (II Corinthians 4:17)? If conflict is necessary to my success, let me accept it gracefully.

Perhaps you are writing a chapter today that is laced with bitter conflict. Betrayal? Slander? Crushing failure? Poverty? Grief? Write on, comrade. Resolution will come at book's end when "ye shall receive a crown of glory that fadeth not away" (I Peter 5:4).

"Why do writers so seldom look back to the Old Masters to learn more about their craft?"
—Marshall in <u>Writer's Digest</u>

Chapter Six

Cure for Writer's Block ✍

W hat next? Where do I go from here? Help! I'm out of words, inspiration and ideas!

For every writer there is a fear that far outstrips deadlines, a stroke or an IRS audit. It is a blank page accompanied by a blank mind. We call it the "blank page phobia." There is nothing scarier.

"Every writer is susceptible to this syndrome, which may be manifested by a dearth of ideas, a state of self-dissatisfaction, or an inability to organize," says the *Writer's Encyclopedia.*

You might compare the feeling to sitting in a car with a dead battery and four flat tires. Or fishing in a pond with no water. Or trying to make cookies with no flour, eggs or sugar.

Haunting my mind is a time–after writing for weeks –that I was certain I had used up every adjective, every adverb, every noun in the universe. I would never be able to write another page, for there would never be the material for another page.

What I didn't realize is that I had only depleted *my own little world.* There were plenty more resources beyond myself if I would dig them out, resources that could supply what my own mind lacked. To have the gold, though, I would have to pan for it. It wouldn't leap into my pocket.

Do you ever feel at a standstill in your spiritual life? You've said everything you know to say in prayer. You sing the same songs to the same soap suds every morning as you clean the kitchen. You feel stale and used up. Where to from here? What next?

You have spiritual writer's block. But don't panic. There is a cure for it!

The cure is reaching beyond yourself, getting out of your mental rut. Study! Research! Learn!

Research is anything you do to learn about a subject. Ask. Seek. Knock. "Martyr yourself if you have to in researching your subject," advises a literary agency. If reading and searching and digging is necessary to an earthly writer, how much more important should it be to a writer of soul matters?

To write one of my books, I needed to know about early aviation. My own knowledge registered a little above zero. From the library I checked out books. And more books. And still more books. I acquainted myself with the history of the Wright brothers; Charles Lindbergh, who made the first trans-Atlantic flight; and pioneer military pilots from World War I and World War II. I met the experts on the pages of those books. I listened to them talk, explain and inform me about airplanes, their origins and their progress.

Hard work? Absolutely! Time consuming? Horribly! Wearisome? An understatement! Research is light years removed from my favorite pastime, but it is necessary. It adds richness, depth to any piece of literature. Someone has said, "The difference between me and an expert is research."

I want to be the best Christian I can be, but I sometimes run out of inspiration. Where can I go to jump start my brain?

We are all aware that the Bible is the lodestar of all resources for our books of life, supplying information and inspiration in abundance. I cannot afford to neglect my study of the Bible. But there are other effectual sources as well. Ladies retreats. Camps. Tapes. Books.

If your faith has writer's block, read some of the histories of our forefathers. Need a miracle? Read *Old Time Preacher Man.* You'll learn about a young Christian early in the twentieth century who needed food. He prayed, and as a bread truck rounded the corner at an intersection, a loaf of bread tumbled off and rolled right toward him! Now tie that story with the Bible's "Jesus Christ the same yesterday, and to day, and for ever" (Hebrews 13:8).

Need a healing? Read the marvelous accounts of healing in *God Answers Prayer*. Then match those testimonies with "for I am the LORD that healeth thee" (Exodus 15:26).

The "Old Masters" can point us to spiritual writing techniques that are timeless. Review their biographies, and you will find insights into prayer, fasting and sacrifice. Study their songs. One of their favorites held this line: "Get your knees acquainted with the cold and rocky ground." (Our knees are hardly acquainted with the carpet, much less the ground.) That was their secret. Total dedication. Should we wonder that their books of life were blockbusters for Jesus?

Study the pioneers' unwavering trust with a magnifying glass. Their simple language. Their sincerity. See how they stuck to their convictions and how they shunned anything with the dust of the world about it–medicine shows, carnivals, rodeos, skating rinks. Ask questions. Listen to the best of their hearts.

What better resource could you find to enrich your own story or to inspire you to start another chapter? They left us big shoes to fill, but the path that led them to victory will lead us there, too.

I chanced upon an article about six top-selling authors of the early 1900s. Of a writer named Gardner, whose sales exceeded 135 million, it was said, "His story was literally *everything* to him." From Mr. Gardner I learned a valuable truth. The story that I am writing for God–my Christian walk–must mean everything to me. More than my own ambitions. More than my loved ones. More than life itself. To have a sell-out edition for my Lord requires that I be sold out to Him.

The next author was credited for knowing and loving every character in his book. Oh, what a lesson! Do I love each person I meet in my walk through life?

The third "made the impossible become possible" in his book. He leaves us believing that dreams can come true when we utilize the often unnoticed resources available to us. His characters scorn the humdrum, mundane routines, determined to do and to be what they once only dreamed of. I have dreamed of giving a Bible study. Why not? A dreamer that I met tacked up an advertisement in a grocery store: "Free Bible with every Bible study." It worked.

Of the fourth, a 45 million book seller, the reviewer said you read this writer's book to get to the end, hoping the end would be worth the time you spent. "You don't read a book to get to the middle," he pointed out. "You read a book to get to the end. It's got to be totally satisfactory in the last line." Every word, every sentence, every paragraph in our lives must be geared to a successful conclusion. That's what writing–and living–are all about.

The fifth author, who had his works translated into fourteen languages, owed his success to his ability to live in the moment and see that all his characters did the same. One could not recall his characters without recalling how they were dressed, how they spoke and all the other ways they interacted with their world. Godliness is a day in and day out project.

The last, known to his readers as Robbins, had "staying power." He started out as a lowly grocery boy but kept plugging until (it was claimed) one of his books sold every minute. "He never let his readers down," was the report. The lesson we can learn from Robbins is self-evident, summed up in a single word: *Faithfulness* to the cause.

As spiritual writers, we can study the countless masterpieces of yesterday–those masterpieces that excited and moved their readers–to get patterns for our own lives. We could probably borrow a few strokes from those bygone masters for a bestseller of our own.

Many of our "Old Masters" could say with Christ, "For I have given you an example, that ye should do as I have done. . . ." (John 13:15). Indeed, we have a rich heritage, worthy of our research.

When I have exhausted my own supply, when faith, hope and charity have leaked through the cracks and my mental cabinet is empty, and when I sit staring at a blank page in my life's book, what then? I burrow into some wonderful resources, borrowing faith from Abraham, patience from Job, wisdom from Daniel, zeal from Paul and revelation from John.

Goodbye, blank page phobia. . . .

"Most writers expect a certain amount of cleanup and correction during the editorial process and are grateful for it."
—Selected

Chapter Seven

The Editor

O h (shudder), where would I be without a good editor? No, don't tell me. It's too awful.

I need an editor. I must have an editor.

In my lifetime I have met self-made writers who don't want their work edited by anybody. They can't abide the changing of a single word, comma or spelling from the original creation. They can't bear criticism, however valuable or necessary. That is why their books seldom "fly."

Thank God, I have a merciless editor, my daughter. She should have been an English professor. No, on second thought, she shouldn't have been. No one would have passed her class! (Just kidding.)

She is honest with me, threatening me with dire consequences if I let a page go to a higher power without her careful scrutiny. She is, doubtless, the reason for some thirty of my books on the Christian market. I wouldn't take all the gold in Fort Knox for her.

Now, here is the clincher right up front. YOUR PASTOR IS YOUR SPIRITUAL EDITOR. "Obey them that have the rule over you, and submit yourselves: for they watch for your souls, as they that must give account, that they may do it with joy, and not with grief: for that is unprofitable for you" (Hebrews 13:17).

Editing is the art of making material suitable for publication. Editors decide what should be added or deleted to improve and enhance the text. They are the "gatekeepers" of publishing. An editor works with the author and approves the book for publishing. All successful publishing companies hire editors. It is vitally important to have a thorough editor.

(If you will insert "pastor" where I say "editor," you will ferret out the message I am trying to convey.)

An editor reads the manuscript line by line, word by word and is charged with preparing the book for print. This means correcting errors–spelling, grammar, definition, usage, fact–and styling the text for consistency.

The editor's job is to head off failure. Your pastor knows that your life's book must comply with heaven's standards, or it will not be accepted by the Publisher. Always remember that a good editor is your friend, working for your good. It is his responsibility to see that the book of your life remains true to its outline and fulfils the Publisher's goals for the book. His job is a difficult one because he is seldom supervising only one book at a time.

What does an editor look for? Zondervan Publishers prints a list of editorial considerations. One of their first questions is, "Is the focus clear?"

A pastor wants each of his writers focused on spiritual matters. "Let this mind be in you, which was also in Christ Jesus" (Philippians 2:5). Being spiritually minded is not just for Sundays or Wednesday nights but for every day.

Sometimes my daughter/editor calls to say, "I'm sorry, Mother, but you will have to rewrite this entire paragraph. Your meaning isn't clear." (In her words, "Mother, this doesn't make sense!") She detects inaccuracies and ambiguities that would confuse readers and distract them from a full understanding of the text. Often the presence or absence of punctuation can entirely change the tenor of a sentence. My dear editoress, trained for close textual reading, calls on me to clarify my work. Together, she and I verify exactly what I want to say.

This tedious effort to locate and eliminate all the "bugs" in my manuscript may cost me a few hours of time, but the success of my work rests on it. Working patiently with my editor, my chances of producing a printworthy book are multiplied manyfold.

A pastor doesn't ask us to make changes just for the

sport of it. It would be much easier for him to gloss over our errors, but he wants our books to be accepted. As the *Writer's Market* explains, virtually no book is accepted 100 percent as is by the publisher. It is the writer's job to write but the editor's job to edit. Never resent your editor/pastor. He is trying to help you to produce the best book you can!

In the *Writer's Standard of Practice* is this pledge: "If the editor has misunderstood, I will politely point this out only if in so doing my manuscript then may prove acceptable to him. Nor will I argue with any comment volunteered by him."

A good, working relationship with one's editor is of inestimable value. When he makes a note in the margin, "Tighten this up," get busy! The success or failure of your life's book could well hinge on his suggestions.

Paul reminds us in Ephesians 4:12 and 13 that God gave us pastors "for the perfecting of the saints, for the work of the ministry, for the edifying of the body of Christ: Till we all come in the unity of the faith, and of the knowledge of the Son of God, unto a perfect man, unto the measure of the stature of the fulness of Christ." No, this isn't an easy task.

In the earliest of my writings, I made a bundle of blunders. I dipped in and out of the minds of all the characters in my stories. I told what he thought, what she thought and what everyone else thought as the narrative conglomerated into a muddled mess. (How could I get into *everybody's* minds?) An editor, a brave soul, kindly suggested that I stick with the thoughts of one character at a time. I was thrilled that he took the time to instruct me! I'll always love him for it.

That's the way I feel about my pastor. I am grateful for his instructions, corrections and suggestions. "All scripture is given by inspiration of God, and is profitable for doctrine, for reproof, for correction, for instruction in righteousness: That the man of God may be perfect, throughly furnished unto all good works" (II Timothy 3:16,17).

I may have to revise. And revise. And revise. I may have to cut, lengthen or strengthen my story. But I want to produce the best spiritual book possible for my Lord.

An author who had just found a lucrative niche with his first book said, "There are people along the way who can help you improve your writing. Listen to them carefully. My book was immeasurably improved by the gentle advice of my copy editor, who was by far the most important person in the entire process."

I hope that you are blessed with a good editor/pastor. I am. He is putting the final, polishing touches on my manuscript before he lays it in God's hands.

"Let the elders that rule well be counted worthy of double honour, especially they who labour in the word and doctrine" (I Timothy 5:17).

And They All Lived Happily Ever After

Thanks, Pastor. *Double* thanks!

"The clearest and most subtle means of presenting character is through dialogue."
—<u>The Writer</u>

Chapter Eight

Who Said What? ✍🏻

In one writing class, the teacher gave us an experimental assignment. We were told to write a story with no quotes. No one talked to anyone else. Straight narrative.

Then we were instructed to take that same story and rewrite it with dialogue, our characters talking to one another.

Guess which was the most interesting? You guessed it! The conversational one. Dialogue–the voice of your characters–is the life of your story. The writer vanishes, and his characters come alive. Dialogue shows the heart of your characters so that your readers may identify with them.

If I pick up a book with stretches of long, boring paragraphs, I soon cast it aside or skip down to a patch of lively conversation. You probably do that same thing unless you are captivated by monotonous detail.

How can we relate this to our spiritual books? Our books of life must "talk" to those who read them if we are to be effective witnesses. The world isn't interested in long blocks of narration or even in long, detailed sermons. They want to see a Christian in action. Walking. Talking. Caring. Living his/her religion.

They want to see reaction, too. What do we say when we are reviled? Being reviled, we bless (I Corinthians 4:12). When we are persecuted? We suffer it (same verse). When we are defamed? We intreat (next verse).

We want our readers–our neighbors, friends, and family–to see Christ. A Georgia writer says, "One thing I strive for in my writing is to remove *self* from the picture and give a gift the world will be able to relate to."

Our theme is Jesus. He is the focal point of our lives' books. He is the hero. To make your Hero live in the minds of your readers, move into His thoughts and feelings. Say what He would say. Try to think as He would think. Try to react as He would react. "Let this mind be in you, which was also in Christ Jesus" (Philippians 2:5).

An important reminder in our class study was this: Watch that a secondary character does not upstage your main character. The cares of life would like to allocate Jesus to a secondary position and to sabotage the success of our story. We can't let that happen.

Do I put my family before the Lord? My friends? My companion? When visitors come, do I stay home from church? Do I fail to pray when other interests call? Where are my priorities? "And he is before all things, and by him all things consist. And he is the head of the body, the church: who is the beginning, the firstborn from the dead; that in all things he might have the preeminence" (Colossians 1:17,18).

"No good book will ever proceed from a superficial mind," Henry James believed. It was his conviction that the writer of a book should be a composition of the best and most honorable things, not presuming to portray heroic men unless he was praiseworthy himself.

In short, we cannot produce spiritual books with carnal lifestyles. "For to be carnally minded is death; but to be spiritually minded is life and peace" (Romans 8:6).

"A writer must be completely honest and sincere," another master of the pen said. The false-hearted are automatically eliminated. They are weighed in the balance and found unworthy to be entrusted with the thoughts of God. Great dialogue in our spiritual books requires a right perspective toward life, toward mankind and toward God.

"Tell me your writing secrets, and I'll pay you well," a businessman said to a college teacher.

"Write to express and not to impress," said the teacher, "and don't be self-indulgent. A writer should not be seen."

We are writing to express Christ to the world and not to impress the world with ourselves. Our ego should never intrude. ". . . I live; yet not I, but Christ liveth in me. . . ." (Galatians 2:20). Let the "who said what" be His voice.

The Bible's most fascinating stories are written in dialogue. Parables. The temptation of Jesus. The trial of Jesus. Peter's message on the Day of Pentecost.

I have a red letter edition of the Bible, and I like to read the "red," the dialogue of my Lord. May my book of life be an extension of His ministry.

Chapter Nine

Keep On Keeping On ✍

Two ingredients . . . If I were submitting a recipe for an author, I would include the two items in equal amounts. Persistence and a thick skin.

One year in the '80s I barely covered my postage. It seems to my sketchy memory that I cleared 84 cents. Not quite enough to turn in to the IRS. I sent out, uh, maybe forty projects. I sold four.

I shipped items to magazines all over the USA and got rejection slips from all over the USA. I got so many of the deplorable documents that I made a "rejection" file. Before long, those impersonal form letters didn't even bother me. I came to expect them.

I tried everything I knew to get in print. I wrote from the single character viewpoint, from the multiple character viewpoint, in the first person, third person and in no person at all. I counted words and pored over market lists. I tried kids' stories, junior stories, youth stories and adult stories. I submitted fiction and nonfiction. I even tried a poem or two. I double spaced and measured margins and (by faith) put my Social Security number at the top of the page. Still no luck.

The rejection slips had all sorts of preprinted data, but the most frequently checked box was this: Your story/article/item does not fit our publishing needs at this time. Translated into English, that means, "We don't want it."

But I didn't give up. Out there somewhere was somebody who did want it.

Almost all great writers, according to a back issue of *Guide to Getting Published*, have had their works rejected. "You have to pull yourself together," the article stated, "and try again."

(Don't give up; we are headed for a spiritual application.) A story entitled "I Can Climb Higher Than You" was rejected forty-seven times. When, on the forty-eighth submission, it was accepted, it won Best Story of the Year from one of the same magazines that had rejected it!

(Here it comes.) Some folks, with a first rejection, are devastated. "I'm not good enough," they grouse. They put away their spiritual books and close the drawers. They have forgotten Paul's "And let us not be weary in well doing: for in due season we shall reap, if we faint not"

(Galatians 6:9).

(Here it is.) So you didn't make the choir? The chorale? You didn't win the election as team leader, Ladies Division president or youth pastor? Keep writing! "To every thing there is a season, and a time to every purpose under the heaven," says wise Solomon in Ecclesiastes 3:1.

A rejection is nothing more than a signal to work harder, to try again. "Never interpret rejections as a failing grade," an author from the 1970s who sold her book in the high six figures says. "Just keep going." When her book was returned to her with unkind remarks, she paid not a whit of attention to the insults. She kept writing, kept improving. "You just have to do your best," she concluded, "and keep believing in yourself."

A successful writer picks up his pen and writes again after rejection. He writes whether or not he feels like writing. He doesn't let yesterday's disappointment pull a cloud over today's hope.

Persistence. That's writing in our books of life when it's hot. When it's cold. When it's easy. When it's hard. When we're liked. When we're disliked. Waiting until you are "in the mood" to write is a luxury a spiritual writer cannot afford. Nor can you wait for a "great inspiration." Real writers know that inspiration is another word for hard work.

Persistence. A drug addict and alcoholic from

Alabama who had been broke and unemployed for six months picked up the pieces of his life and wrote his book. His only advice to other writers is, "Never give up."

Weary Christian, forget the past. Forget your mistakes. Forget all those "rejection slips." We have beautiful books to write! "Brethren, I count not myself to have apprehended: but this one thing I do, forgetting those things which are behind, and reaching unto those things which are before, I press toward the mark for the prize of the high calling of God in Christ Jesus" (Philippians 3:13,14).

What would have happened it I had thrown in the towel when I received my first letter of rejection thirty books ago? What will happen if I put aside my spiritual book of life when I face rejection? I will miss the greatest of all rewards: my Great Publisher's words at book's end. "Well done . . ."

"But he that shall endure to the end, the same shall be saved" (Matthew 24:13).

Chapter Ten

Tools of the Trade ✍🏻

Raised eyebrows. Not so subtle hints. Obsolete ribbons. Nothing can unglue me from my trusty, old, standard typewriter.

Why do I cling to it? Because it has never let me down. Electricity goes out, computers get glitches and outlets don't grow on trees. But with my backdated standard, I can pound away on the creek bank, five miles from modern conveniences.

Long ago I discovered that all writers are blessed with friends and cursed with enemies. Not *people* friends and enemies, but those abstract angels and devils like outlines, proofs and machinery. Tools of the trade.

I also discovered that different writers have different friends and enemies. What might set a trap for me might not bother you at all and vice versa. As I mentioned, my old standard is a real friend. I appreciate its white-key smile each morning. It is a loyal Royal. I'm glad to leave the 99 Windows to someone else.

My Number 2 yellow pencil is a friend, too. I can take my spiral notebook with me to the hospital, to the hunting lodge or to the restaurant. I don't want to miss any thoughts "on the run." Mental ink fades fast. I can do the "splash it all over the page" first draft with that little, yellow stick.

I'm the same way about my spiritual book. I like to take it with me everywhere I go lest I miss an opportunity to jot down an incident, a blessing, a thought that might otherwise slip away. I can't wait until I get to church (or until there is a revival) to do all my "writing."

"Therefore we ought to give the more earnest heed to the things which we have heard, lest at any time we should let them slip" (Hebrews 2:1).

Most of my tools are well worn and time proven. The front cover is off my hard-backed dictionary. I hate to part with it for a new one; it has been a true friend.

It reminds me of my old Scoffield Bible, the one my mother bought for me on my sixteenth birthday. Its leather is worn to a frazzle, but I still love it. I have had several since in various sizes and colors, and now I'm ready for one with larger print. But the markings in that dear, old "original" still make my heart beat faster!

I bought a *Describer's Dictionary* at B. Dalton Bookstore because I wanted to make description my friend.

(It was my enemy at the time.) It seemed to me that detail simply filled good space that could be better employed. Why does a house have to be huge, white, freshly painted, windowed, porched and proud? Let's find out what's in that house! I'm as uncomfortable with dead space as a radio announcer is with dead air. It makes me a nervous wreck! I write telegram style. "She smiled. STOP. He smiled back. STOP. She fainted. STOP."

In classes that hounded, "cut back, cut back," I struggled with an unconventional problem. When I finished my story, I had a poor, transparent skeleton that needed some meat on his bones. Why bother with details?

Now, for a station break: Details are important to God. Ask Moses what a couple of extra swats on the rock cost him. Ask Saul what the sparing of a few sheep and cows lost him. Ask the Children of Israel what a daub of blood on the facing of a door spared them.

God wants details included in our books of life. Details like visits to the prayer room. Punctuality to His house. Honesty on our income tax. Kindness to our neighbors. Godly attire even on vacation.

We rush through life telegram style, cutting corners on things that don't seem to matter, not realizing that we are shortchanging our books. If we are not careful, there won't be enough righteousness recorded to make them acceptable on Judgment Day.

I have another tool that I couldn't live without. That

is my filing cabinet. How cluttered my desk would become if I didn't have a place to file papers that are no longer current! If it is nothing more than a cardboard box, every writer needs a nook in which to stow things.

Ah, if we could learn this lesson in our walks with God! We clutter our lives with too many rough drafts from the past. File them, and work on your new and current chapter! You haven't room for yesterday's rejections or successes on your "desk." Don't let things stack. So three chapters back you suffered an injury? Forget it, and write on.

Take a hint from the apostle Paul. "The life which I *now* live," he said, "I live by the faith of the Son of God" (Galatians 2:20) (emphasis mine). Paul kept his book up to date.

What other tools (some now quite obsolete) kept me writing through the years? One was correction fluid. I used bottles of it. I inhaled so much of the goop that it is a wonder I'm not brain damaged. Today, making corrections is swift and easy. Just hit the delete button. No sweat. No time. No white-out.

Sounds a lot like modern day repentance, doesn't it? No restitution. No anguish. No apologies to God or man. Careless living is no problem. It is quickly erased and forgotten, omitted from the screen. No "white-out" for sins, no covering, for they are not sins at all. They are only minor mistakes.

I know little about computers, but I am told that nothing is ever truly deleted. The data lurks somewhere in the internal mechanism of the machine and can be retrieved with the right formula. I want my sins covered by the blood of Jesus! I don't want them lurking in the internal mechanism of my spirit, summoned forth by the Judge of all on the Day of Reckoning. "Blessed is he whose transgression is forgiven, whose sin is covered" (Psalm 32:1).

Yes, there are some basics you will need for your spiritual writing business. Spiritual tools. What are they? Holiness. Selflessness. Godliness. His Word. His Name. His Spirit. They've been used for generations, but they still work.

"Forasmuch as ye are manifestly declared to be the epistle of Christ . . . written not with ink, but with the Spirit of the living God. . . ." (II Corinthians 3:3).

"'All rights' means a writer forfeits his right to sell to another publisher."

—L.M.

Chapter Eleven

Of Writers and Rights

I ran my finger slowly down the long lists of publishers, bypassing all those that required an author to grant them "all rights." (The Big Publishers.) I wanted to send my amateur stories, which weren't worth an editor's efforts anyway, to various small markets, hoping to sell the same story several times. That way I would make more money, or so I thought. But I soon learned that I didn't have the correct concept about rights.

Had my work been accepted by the Big Publisher– the "all rights" publisher–I would have gained more income than I did with all the small presses put together. Most of the small presses paid a paltry sum if anything. Some paid with copies of their magazines.

As a spiritual writer, how much of your "rights" are you willing to offer to God? Each writer must decide that for himself. That is the right of the writer.

In the publishing world, there are "first serial rights." That means that a writer offers the publisher the privilege of using his or her material for the first time. Thereafter, the writer snatches back his rights for himself. Sounds like some Christians, doesn't it?

Then there are "one time rights." The publisher has no guarantee that he is the first in line. He can only use the material once. Then the writer takes his work elsewhere. (To church on Easter and to the lake thereafter?)

There are "second serial rights," too. These are also known as reprint rights. The first work has been given to someone else, decreasing the value of the article since it isn't an exclusive submission. As the writer's work has been used previously, the writer usually benefits only half from these rights. Half-hearted Christians give the first rights to their lives to the world, money, or other cares. Their worth to God is decreased drastically since He is not at liberty to use them as He would like, and they benefit little from their part-time service to God.

"Simultaneous rights"–the ones I wasted so much time and energy on–give the writer the option to send his freelance literature anywhere and everywhere. He can submit the same article to a dozen different places. This is, according to the *Writer's Market*, relegated primarily to

74

religious magazines.

Editors hate simultaneous submissions and with good reason. After weeks of analyzing, an editor might be dismissed by the writer for another with a more lucrative offer. (Remembering that editors are pastors in our analogy, you will unravel the cryptoquote here quite clearly.)

Because of the exclusive nature of their company, top paying publishers insist on *all rights*. They flatly refuse to accept a manuscript for consideration if other publishers are also considering it. A writer who agrees to this all rights contract cannot send his material elsewhere. He signs over the copyright to the company publishing his work.

Have you found yourself? God, the Great Publisher, will only accept all rights. Don't bother to send Him a simultaneous submission or one time rights. He isn't interested in sometime Christians or part-time Christians. It is all or none with Him.

"No man can serve two masters: for either he will hate the one, and love the other; or else he will hold to the one, and despise the other. Ye cannot serve God and mammon" (Matthew 6:24).

Pastors don't appreciate saints who hop around from church to church. After months of agonizing for their souls, trying to get them "acceptable" to the Publisher, he sees them run somewhere else. Falling under the simultaneous rights heading, they often become "Raging waves of the sea, foaming out their own shame; wandering stars, to whom is reserved the blackness of darkness for ever" (Jude, verse 13). Most pastors learn to recognize these wanderers, and word gets around.

There's yet another right of the writer. He or she can go to a subsidy publisher. These companies, also known as vanity publishers, have proliferated in recent years. Subsidy publishers are self-structured companies for authors who want total control over their own books, who want to do things their own way. These writers have no rules to follow, no format. They don't even have to have an editor. There is no one to correct spelling, punctuation or to proof the writer's work.

It sounds like a fun way to write a book and offers a lot of freedom, doesn't it? Oh, but there are drawbacks! With this sort of publishing, the writer pays for his own book. He chooses his own title. He provides his own cover. He pays the postage. He markets his own book. It is his sole project. For a lot of unfortunate authors, it has been time and money down the drain. According to the *Writer's Encyclopedia*, it is estimated that only one in ten authors ever recoups his investment.

There are subsidy publishers in religion, too. They are proliferating in this end time. From them you may expect inferior workmanship and a great deal of headaches and expense. Paul had some of these "subsidy publishers" in his day. He warned the Ephesians not to be "tossed to and fro, and carried about with every wind of doctrine, by the sleight of men, and cunning craftiness, whereby they lie in wait to deceive" (Ephesians 4:14).

These wolves in sheep's clothing will accept anything you want to write in your life's book and will print it as is. Adultery. Alternate lifestyles. Hypocrisy. No changes necessary. They will ignore the rules of writing because they as hirelings "looketh for the reward of their work" (Job 7:2). Satan is the Editor-in-Chief of all these spiritual vanity companies.

Our cities are dotted with churches where anything goes. No standards, no rules. You don't have to give up anything, submit to any authority or follow any scruples. But in most cases, the writer will awaken to discover he has invested his resources in a cause that will pay no dividends. What he invests, he loses.

The paid printer can take his money and run. He has nothing to lose. It matters not to him what happens to the writer, his work or his future. Such publishers, of course, pay no royalties at all to the author.

"But he that is an hireling, and not the shepherd, whose own the sheep are not, seeth the wolf coming, and leaveth the sheep, and fleeth: and the wolf catcheth them, and scattereth the sheep. The hireling fleeth, because he is an hireling, and careth not for the sheep" (John 10:12,13).

Well, in the matter of my earthly books, I finally decided to turn all rights to a good book publisher. They paid for the cover, the artwork and the printing. They did the distribution and the shipping. They did the advertising and collecting. Only then did I realize any appreciable profit.

I have made the same choice spiritually. My Heavenly Publisher has borne the expense of my life's book. When my book is complete, the *royalty* will be mine.

How can you beat that?

"If you think you've got to string together big fancy words and high-flying phrases, forget it."
—E. T. Thompson

Chapter Twelve

Words or Wordy?

One of my most editor annoying idiosyncrasies is making up my own words. If Mr. Webster can invent words, why not I?

The telephone rings. It is my editor.

"This isn't a word, Mother!" says the voice at the other end.

Awwwwww!

"Therefore, you can't use it."

"Why not?" (Don't ever ask that!)

"Because it isn't a word."

Some words sound great. They look good, but they aren't good because they aren't right. They are not in agreement with the Authority.

In the writing of our lives' books, we cannot invent our own "words" to live by. Some folks suppose because they write something, think something or say something, that makes it right. Not so. We must live by the Word, the Authority.

I like words. They enrich my life with their music, their melody, their drama. I enjoy working with them, playing with them, studying with them. I am eager to meet new ones, to coax the bashful ones out of hiding and to consult the silver-haired veterans, searching my word finder.

Now and then I try a big, important sounding word, sometimes relocating it completely out of its environment and into foreign territory. My editor seldom appreciates my ten dollar words. She thinks no one would know what "hippocrepiform" means, so she prefers that I simply say "horseshoe shaped." She liked "wrinkled" more than "rugose." She would much rather have me simplify and clarify than have me soaring high above the crowd, singing like an icteridae . . . er, a bird. She concurs with Paul, who said, "Except ye utter . . . words easy to be understood, how shall it be known what is spoken?" (I Corinthians 14:9).

"The interesting thing about writing is that the world's greatest pen masters use sentences which are almost childlike to convey subjects that are profound," says an article in the *Christian Writer's Guild Starter Kit*. Didn't the Lord say something about our becoming as children?

History holds some examples of the power of simplicity. "To be or not to be?" asks Shakespeare's Hamlet. The longest word contains three letters. The Bible opens with a sentence well within the skills of a brilliant twelve-year-old. "In the beginning God created the heaven and the earth."

A scientist, using scientific jargon, wrote, "The biota exhibited a one hundred percent mortality response." He could have written, "All the fish died."

A speech writer for President Franklin D. Roosevelt wrote, "We are endeavoring to construct a more inclusive society." F.D.R. changed it to, "We're going to make a country in which no one is left out."

Words don't have to be wordy to stand tall. There are an abundance of first degree words that are simple yet powerful. *Come*, Jesus said, and Peter walked on the water. *Come forth*, he commanded, and Lazarus exited the cemetery.

God isn't complicated. The awesomeness of His Book is in its openness that touches our spirits. Consider Psalm 23. "He maketh me to lie down in green pastures." We can feel the tranquility. "He leadeth me beside the still waters." Peace settles over our minds. Elementary words show us that the bedding down place isn't dry and stubbly. It is soft and green. The waters do not roil and froth and tumble. They are calm and still. Picturesque words, aren't they? A word can paint a thousand pictures.

Words also have "sounds." Writers are advised to read aloud what they have written to see how it sounds. Do I sound like a Christian? How does my prayer sound to God? I must take time to listen to myself. "A word fitly spoken is like apples of gold in pictures of silver" (Proverbs 25:11).

Certain clusters sound right. Tall, dark and handsome have an ear pleasing resonance. Have you noticed that in your spiritual book groups of three have a beautiful rhyme and cadence? Righteousness, peace and joy. Faith, hope and charity. Blood, water and Spirit. Father, Word and Holy Ghost.

Words play "follow the leader." When we step out in faith and put down a first, solid statement, other words will follow. Before we know it, delight and enthusiasm are instilled in our daily writings, and our pleasure touches off a corresponding chord in the hearts of others.

Moods are created by words. That is why we should choose words carefully for our books of life. If we choose dark and depressing words, they will fill our pages with gloom. "Nobody appreciates me." "My money never goes far enough." "I have the world's worst mother-in-law."

But if we choose cheerful, faith building words, our pages will be brightened. "Today is a beautiful day!" "God will supply my needs." "Heaven is ahead."

Each morning when I start my page, I list a hundred blessings in my time of prayer. It starts me in a thankful mode, and that sets the mood for my entire day's "writing." Try it.

When I begin a new fiction book for the Christian market, I have no idea what words it will contain. However, it doesn't alarm me. The words usually get there on time. There is nothing truly alarming about not knowing in April what you will be writing in your life's book in August. Write the words that come to you for April, and when August arrives, so will the inspiration.

Apply yourself, and God will help you write your story. Word by word. It's that simple.

"Ideas are plentiful and cheap while the difficult part is taking them to fruition."
—Source Unknown

Chapter Thirteen

The Very Idea! 👌

P lotting. That takes ideas. Plodding. That's what it takes to turn ideas into plots.

Please read the quote above the chapter title about ideas invented by I don't know who. Please understand that the "I don't know who" doesn't know what he's talking about. Ideas plentiful and cheap? Who is kidding whom? If I could nab an idea, I would be delighted to take it to fruition or anywhere else it wanted to go.

I am driven to madness by people who can pick ideas off the top of their hats. Anytime. All the time. Anywhere. Yet I am even more frustrated by the multitudes who do absolutely nothing with their wonderful ideas. At least they could lend them. Or sell them. Or give them away.

Ideas, according to my diagnosis, are unpredictable,

unreasonable, unmerciful and a lot of other "uns." There is no prognosis for their getting any better. No herbs or pain pills or anti-inflammatory medicine will help.

One never knows when or where an idea may appear. Or disappear. The plot for one of my children's stories showed up in a dream one dark night.

Ideas will sneak in while you are trying to study your Sunday School lesson. Or they'll show up at the supermarket while you're reading the label on the cream style corn. Or while you are bent over tying your shoes.

Is there anything more agitating than a naughty child who runs from you and you are not fast enough to catch him? Yes! A brainchild who runs from you when you chase it; that is what ideas do to me. They play hide and seek, and I'm always "it."

A sick feeling of desertion swallowed me (coat and all) after I had submitted the fifth book of the *Bent-Winged Angel* series. The very air around me seemed empty. I had depleted the atmosphere, the stratosphere, yea, the very ionosphere of ideas.

Perhaps they were playing tricks on me. Okay, ideas. Go play your games with someone else. I refuse to grovel at your feet, allowing you to pummel me, torment me, kick me around and then forsake me for someone else. I'm through!

For three months, I spurned the piteous cry of my Number 2 yellow pencil. It was May, and my daughter,

Angella, was graduating from high school. Every bed in the house and travel trailer was filled, double occupancy, and we had borrowed two more trailers.

In the midst of the melee, my father had a massive hemorrhage, and we rushed him to the hospital forty miles away. Then my son had an unclassified attack, and we rushed him there, too.

With two in the hospital and yet wall to wall people at home, I was stretched tighter than the budget. On the way to the hospital, driving alone, I fell in behind a truck. A chain clinked in the bed of that truck, and when it did, something clicked in my mind. An idea. An idea for another book!

The book would begin like this: *"Clink! Clink!* Somewhere inside, Julie heard them break. Chains! Rusted they were (but in no wise weakened) by torrents of tears. Now they fell away of their own accord . . . leaving her free." The book would be entitled *Love's Velvet Chains.*

Why, the very audacity of that idea! I thought. To show up at a time like this. Here I am driving in heavy traffic. I can't write. I don't even have my pencil with me. When I get to the hospital, I still can't write. When I get home, I've people to feed. I can't write!

Could I make notes on the hem of my dress or on the bottom of my shoes? On the palm of my hand? It was as if the idea was mocking me, threatening suicide if I didn't cater to it. Right now.

Is it any wonder that I get exasperated? I woo ideas, pampering and petting them. I wheedle them and cajole them. I can pitch them out, but I know that sooner or later I will crawl after them to make amends. For a writer can't get anywhere without ideas. They are our bloodstream.

Now. Let me suggest the metaphor of this chapter, a point of spiritual reference that you can take with you to help with your book of life. We will always be frustrated and discouraged if we pursue our own ideas. "For my thoughts are not your thoughts, neither are your ways my ways, saith the LORD" (Isaiah 55:8).

God did not intend for us to engineer our own plots. That is His business. "Trust in the LORD with all thine heart; and lean not unto thine own understanding" (Proverbs 3:5). It is His sublime pleasure to provide the theme for our earthly journeys. "For we are his workmanship, created in Christ Jesus unto good works, which God hath before ordained that we should walk in them" (Ephesians 2:10).

Submitting to God's ideas, His will and His thoughts will take the stress from our tasks. Suddenly we realize that we don't have to chase our own fickle ideas. We don't even have to plot our own tomorrows. We are loosed from the Pharaohs who demand that we make our own bricks. Our blood pressure drops to normal!

"Lord, what is your plot and plan for me today?" is

a good first thing in the morning prayer. Then let Him take the lead rope.

"For in him we live, and move, and have our being. . . ." (Acts 17:28).

"The merit of any story is revealed in its resolution."
—L.M.

Chapter Fourteen

The Finishing Touch

*A*nd they all lived happily ever after.

Ah, those seven magic words! The child in each of us still wants the story to end this way.

David wanted his story to conclude thus. "LORD, makes me to know mine end," he requested in his thirty-ninth Psalm. He wanted to know for sure he would live happily ever after.

Unfortunately, not all real life stories have such a nice conclusion. A book can have an ever so nice beginning, but if it hasn't a proper resolution, the author has worked in vain.

In a writing contest sponsored by a trade magazine, one of the judges said, "In general, the biggest problem with all these stories–and the 1,704 entries overall–is the ending. Without an ending, or without the *right* ending, a story reads like a vignette."

To write a bad book takes just as much time and physical effort as writing a good one, observes a columnist in *The Writer.* The only difference is that there is no reward for the bad one.

Good endings don't just appear. There are no true surprise endings. The ending, however abrupt, has been foreshadowed all through the story and is not dependent on some twist of amazing coincidence at the last second. It has been developing naturally for many chapters, and the editor and publisher recognize this fact.

So it is with our lives. We've been working toward the last page since the day we began. "Mark the perfect man, and behold the upright: for the end of that man is peace" (Psalm 37:37).

A good ending leaves readers feeling that the story could have ended no other way. In the conclusion, all the threads of the story are neatly tied into a happy or unhappy ending.

In literature, as in life, there are different types of endings. One type is called a "periscope ending." It does not spell out for the reader what actually happens, but it offers a brief glimpse of what the future holds for the characters in the story. The Book of Acts has a periscope ending. It tells us that Paul dwelt two whole years in his own hired house, preaching the Kingdom of God. We can only imagine the wondrous results.

The Bible has a periscope ending. John gives us a

peek into the future, and the Lord tells us, "Surely, I come quickly."

Another type of ending is the "reader's choice ending," which leaves the reader to supply his own opinion of what the future holds. May our spiritual endings be such that our readers don't have to worry about our futures!

Despite a brilliant start, a weak ending will ruin a story's chances of being accepted by the publisher. Sometimes an author sends a chapter or two that snags the editor's attention, but the finished product is dismissed because the ensuing chapters fade. Our Celestial Publisher tells us, "He that shall endure to the end, the same shall be saved" (Mark 13:13).

The conclusion is the part of the story that matters the most. Ezekiel warns us in chapter 33 of his book that righteousness that is not maintained until the last page will do one no good. "Behold, we count them happy which endure," James says in chapter 5, verse 11 of his epistle. The good chapters will be forgotten if the ending is faulty.

The culmination is the part of the story that readers remember after the book is closed. Dorcas' book seemed to be finished. Her friends stood about, weeping. They were remembering. She made aprons for widows. She made gowns for the elderly. She made coats for children. Her book was filled to her final closure with wonderful benevolences. This is what they remembered when her book was finished although she was given extra chapters.

A writer, therefore, must spend as much time and effort on the ending of his story as he does the beginning or the middle. "Better is the end of a thing than the beginning thereof," says the wise man in Ecclesiastes 7:8.

A good resolution requires planning ahead. A writer may not know the details of that resolution, but before he picks up his pen to write his book, he must determine that his book will have a proper finale.

"If I didn't know the ending of a story, I wouldn't begin," states one author.

If we write our lives' stories according to God's plan, we already know what is beyond the last line here. A wedding. The marriage supper. Streets of gold. Gates of pearl. A mansion.

The apostle Paul's book of life was an impressive volume. The preface wasn't pretty, but after his turn-around, it abounded in glory. As he concludes his life's writing and turns it to the Publisher, he knows the ending is right.

"I have fought a good fight, I have finished my course," said he. "I have kept the faith: Henceforth there is laid up for me a crown of righteousness, which the Lord, the righteous judge, shall give me at that day: and not to me only, but unto all them also that love his appearing" (II Timothy 4:7,8).

If I have written well, I know that when my life's book is finished and placed on the Great Publisher's desk,

I need have no fear. "For . . . we have a building of God, an house not made with hands, eternal in the heavens" (II Corinthians 5:1).

That's the sort of ending I like.

And They All Lived Happily Ever After. . . .